TOMORROW SOMEONE WILL ARREST YOU

Also by Meena Kandasamy

Fiction

The Gypsy Goddess
When I Hit You: Or, the Portrait of the Writer as a Young Wife
Exquisite Cadavers

Poetry

Touch
Ms Militancy

TOMORROW SOMEONE WILL ARREST YOU

Meena Kandasamy

Atlantic Books
London

Published in trade paperback in Great Britain in 2023 by Atlantic Books, an imprint of Atlantic Books Ltd.

10 9 8 7 6 5 4 3 2 1

This publication was made possible by the Akademie der Künste, Berlin in the context of a fellowship by the Young Academy.

AKADEMIE DER KÜNSTE

A CIP catalogue record for this book is available from the British Library.

Trade paperback ISBN: 9781838959029
EBook ISBN: 9781838959036

Printed in Great Britain by TJ Books Ltd, Padstow, Cornwall

Atlantic Books
An imprint of Atlantic Books Ltd
Ormond House
26–27 Boswell Street
London
WC1N 3JZ

www.atlantic-books.co.uk

Dedicated to Amma, Dr Vasantha Kandasamy

For your quiet, fierce strength...
For holding me together after each of my heart-breaks...

CONTENTS

HER LOVERS

HER FRIENDS

HER COUNTRY

DRAMATIS PERSONAE

THE POET lives in language. She deploys words as weapon and caress, they are both jagged protest and an offering made to a lover. She sees the weight of history, unwraps implicit meanings hidden in speech. She has not always given herself to poetry, but here, she returns.

HER COMRADE is steadfast: political, reliable, temperamental. He is THE POET's compass of integrity, her second home. He is impassioned, resolute, idealistic, almost lost. Together, they build shelter, raise children, share a life.

HER LOVERS, men and women, are woven through her life, suspended here in memory:
– The one who taught her to love, to soften herself to love's possibilities, but could not himself commit;
– The demon, the tease, the brute, the all-consuming one who makes the rest of the world disappear;
– The stranger for whom she risks everything, builds layers of caution for one perfect, fleeting night.
All HER LOVERS prefer anonymity. Some of them morph into a single creature in the middle of a line of verse. None of them are imaginary.

HER FRIENDS are considered dangerous, threats to the state. They struggle & think & love together with THE POET: they are her allies in language, their voices joining together in an advancing chorus of rage and rallying cry. In standing up against state terror, HER FRIENDS are termed terrorists.

HER COUNTRY is that land where she is instantaneously considered a troublemaker. The oppressive regime is THE POET's intimate enemy – there is no aspect of life that escapes its rigorous incursions, its sanctioned oppressions. Under this rising fascism, THE POET dodges arrest. She also rebels with the certainty that her incarceration is imminent. She inhabits an inversion of her own making: she is guarded with her words; she is reckless in the frontlines of protest. HER COUNTRY is a dream colouring itself. HER COUNTRY is, at this instant, a nightmare.

THE POET

A POEM IN WHICH SHE REMEMBERS

We were not lovers, we were love.
— Jeanette Winterson

The woman you once knew
will not own up to her face.

She'll tie her hair in a topknot,
guard its million tangles, skip
kohl that once defined her eyes,
forsake the loud jewellery, milk
cigarettes in her mouth, and stop
herself from dancing in the rain.

She'll curse her restless anklets
that break the silence of cruel days,
bury herself under a blanket that
betrays the shame of night hungers,
and sleep herself to a dream
of waking by your side.

She'll write you the daring first lines
of long love-letters she will never
send, struggle to prevent a poem
from forming in her mouth,
and in its place, feed the promises
of your kisses to her eager tongue.

I DO NOT KNOW DEATH

I do not know
death, how it feels,
or how long it lasts,
but sometimes think
that when it comes,
it will burn like this
emptiness that follows
the night of your silence—
slow-motion charring,
the refusal to let go
of stillness, and, in
cold blood, the feeding
of its endless hunger
with the panic
in my flesh.

A WILD WOMAN ON A WORD HUNT

Find me another word
that is not so ready. I want
a word that waits and weeps
and hesitates, that knows
of other words I kill, and
grows afraid to take its place.

Find me a word that has heard
of a woman afraid of losing a man
she does not have, find me a word
that flinches at the thought of being
trapped, a word that shows me
stealing time, not men.

Find me a word that is not so safe.
A word for a woman in a forest
to wake up with, a woman who
knows heat and long silences
and sleepless nights, a woman
who works with only words.

Not love, dear poet.
Find me another word.

HOW CAREFUL WAS I WHEN I TOOK MY WAY

Life can only be understood backwards;
but it must be lived forwards.
                    —Søren Kierkegaard

In a lovers' quarrel, questions
come without correct answers.
Which of us broke off what we shared?
In my version of our story, you turned away.
In your version, I was the one who left.

The blank page
holds the definite answer,
and a promise:

I return to you—
And, poetry returns to me.

A SAPPHIC SCAR

1

At _____ , a fellow Indian writer I looked up to, declared,
'You are not bisexual until you've *slept* with a woman'
when I shyly confided in her – several years my senior,
and a lesbian (at that point in time) – that I desired
both men and women.

I felt embarrassed. This felt like the mouth-sores of scurvy,
the weak-soft bones of rickets: a deficiency, a deformity.
I had only one lover in the picture (at that point in time).
But this could be rectified soon I thought, so I let it slip.

I waited for a woman who would ask me out (at that point
    in time).

※ ※

2

She also told me, another day, that my presence on the
writing program was 'denominational'.

She said without saying in as many words that I was there
because I was low-caste, that I came from the margins,
that I was picked out because I was different,
that I served institutional purposes of diversity.

Poets can employ one word to contain a universe of
    meaning.

Denominational meant that I checked some boxes.
Denominational meant that I did not have talent.
Denominational meant that I did not have merit.
Denominational meant that I did not deserve to be there.

Denominational meant that I was not one of them,
meant that I was not one of the Brahmins,
one of those who were born with talent and merit,
one of those whom our religion ordained
intellectually superior by birth.

Even when I was taken in by white people,
I was set apart by the standards of my people.

She *could* have called me token.
If this were happening back home,
she *would* have called me: quota,
category, reservation candidate.

This was a barb older than time, older than pronouns.
This was not about a particular point in time.
A perennial stigma cannot be undone.

Sleeping around/sleeping with/not sleeping at all
does not solve this insult.
Waiting for a woman, or a man,
or a roomful of lovers, does not help either.

Denominational is a deficiency that medicine cannot fix.
Denominational is a deformity that surgery cannot touch.

Being seen as denominational sets me alight,
makes me write word after word in rage,
leave behind this body of work,
so that someday, in another time,
someone else will read me and say:
she deserved her place.

THE SEVEN STAGES

Notes to self: Don't lose him. Don't lose yourself. Don't lose.
Note to lover: Remember this. Nothing else will matter soon.
Note to my readers: Take up this dream. Turn it on its head.
HUB. UNS. ISHQ. AQUIDAT. IBAADAT. JUNOON. MAUT.
These are the seven stages of love in another tongue but
some dark men from my land have lived through this as
if poetic delineation in Arabic was based on Tamil souls.
It always starts with a silent man
locking eyes with a talkative girl
prone to sudden smiles. Attraction
turns to infatuation turns into love
quite quickly. That's the fluff of films
then society intervenes with its caste
codes: sequesters her separates them.
Robbed of two years and two million
kisses, this longing turns to reverence
and worship and obsession. The lovers
rebel, they elope, they marry, they live
like rabbits: delicate and lovely; mostly
underground and always making love.
Soon discovered, they are slaughtered.
They dared to defy but ended up dead.
Take up this dream, turn it on its head.

A CAT CLOSING HER EYES

Poonai kanmoodi kondaal,
Poolokam irundu vidaathu
When a cat shuts its eyes,
the world does not turn dark.

It is said that mothers
have a proverb for every occasion—
amma recycled the same one
to see me through everything.

To tackle my teenage tantrums
Poonai kanmoodi kondaal...
Your sulking does not affect me, girl!

To combat my depression
Poonai kanmoodi kondaal...
Just stop wallowing in your sorrows, girl!

To stop me giving up
Poonai kanmoodi kondaal...
The world will move on without you, girl!

Most of all, to put me together,
heartbreak after heartbreak
Poonai kanmoodi kondaal...
He doesn't see you, girl, you are beautiful,
men will find you, and you will find love!

Sometimes I was the cat,
Sometimes I was the world.
This cat made me loved, unloved,
left me in the lurch, and often,
led me to the light.

A POEM ON NOT WRITING POEMS

These days I write nothing
except my eyes, why share
my drugs of angst or absolute
godlessness when the price,
they have said, will have to be
paid in blood, why speak of meat
or beef, when the aftertaste of talk
is not just a threat of televised gang-rape,
but a village gathering to slaughter a man,
again, why force fit my words to capture
the state, its terror, this state of terror
when friends who planned to read Marx
had prison cells waiting for them, so why
risk, why run for dear life, why rage at all?

'What cannot be said must be suppressed.'
'Why show the scar on your thigh to strangers?'
Lessons I once learnt in my bedroom
are lessons for life.

So, in lamp black, I only write my eyes
in the ritual way some Tamil women
draw a kolam each day, rice flour
out sparkling the early morning sun,
rigid dots anchoring snaking lines, all discipline
a deception to hide the wildness, all symmetry
an excuse for keeping count.

Watch a woman's hands
dance an intricate design,
learn that it's her desire
that she is pouring out
on her doorstep. Like her,
this woman in the mirror
is a woman who pretends
to know her place. Each
night, she washes her eyes,
unwraps her word-wounds,
takes them to bed. At daybreak
she applies a fresh dressing.

HER COMRADE

A SILENT LETTER

We met halfway, in English,
a habit than a language,
precise as bullets in your politics
raw as a knife wound in my poetry.

You, bathing every English word
in your mother tongue, as if this was
the only way of settling down.
You, switching to French in pain,
the sudden *pardon*, the unexpected *oui*
that tells me you were dreaming,
tells me that you have touched ground.

How do I come to your home?

In that land of words where I handcraft
my dreams, we do not have alphabets
that disappear into silences. Not for us
the unspoken sibilants, the gliding liquids,
an elision at the end of words,
contortions of sophistication.

Our vowels, we call them life
our consonants, we treat them as the body
where this life begins to breathe, makes meaning,
makes love, makes do. Everything is meant
to be pronounced. Here, the only rule:
what you see is what you say—
nothing seen goes unsaid.

I struggle with a tongue tied to its roots,
untrained to let things slide, that does not
know to suppress sound, that is dying
to come home to you, instead, stays
a stranger at your door.

VISA GODS

In this story, Eurydice is dark & deadly
& has lived all her life in Hades.
In this story, Orpheus plays the drums.

A ~~semester at sea program~~ Tamil refugee
solidarity group makes them meet.
Orpheus is ensnared watching the way
she talks with her hands and laughs
with her eyes and speaks with an accent
he has never taken to bed. Skin sun-kissed
as cinnamon stick, long hair that anchors storms,
a mouth filled with the coarsest curses on land.
Gossip says it was the spice in her meals,
it may well have been the sex.

For the sake of this story, Orpheus
has to bring her into the first world.
In his contract with the overlords
there's no clause about looking back,
about trust, about hearing the footsteps
of the loved one before walking ahead—
that is not a white people thing at all.

Here, Orpheus must leave.
Eurydice must follow.

In other words, Eurydice,
to smuggle their love,
must screw her way
into Europe.

Eurydice must cross the seas,
pass through border controls,
fight for a Schengen, chant
prayers for her visa, borrow
recklessly with her bank, get
her passport stamped. She
must do this six hundred
times over a lifetime.

Hostage to nation-state, our man
Orpheus must wait, must will himself
to live for a woman who weeps when
she is away, weeps when it's time
to leave, weeps when she cannot
come, who weeps in his arms
because their love story
is not in their hands.

Orpheus no longer plays the drums.

Now, there is no music in his life—
only the silence at parting,
the white noise of waiting.

FINDING YOU

you think you can retreat into a silence

pull away from him, his open smiles
and take back what you have given,
gather whatever is left of you – first,
an instinct to run from harm, halting
speech which descends to still a room,
all that knowledge of playing men. . .
this coy preference for silences, your
skin's desire for the rain-drenched air
of monsoon nights. old superstitions you
cannot grow out of, and, a handful of tamil
endearments you jealously own & fiercely
guard. the recurrent barefoot dream of running
along beaches, and yes, that shameless, reckless
abandon of your screams.

you think these fragments are all you need.
you can make a heap in a corner, open
an instruction manual, and build back
the patchwork doll that you will be, become
full person again, in an elemental state,
extracted into essence, free from the many
faults of your man's presence. all you.
you, given back, to you, at last.

try this sometime. try this now.

you might save yourself, escape
the weight of old scars, find all
the space you will ever need. . .

never stop to tell me how it goes.

i am a traitor to my cause, i am
that woman who weeps for love,
the one who feels lost when
she finds herself alone.
to me, the fire-walk,
the knife-dance, and
the burning, sudden
tears will do.

THE WARS COME HOME

These days I do not read the news.
I stay at home, all day, every day,
dream of monsoons back home
as London rains on my window.

I watch my baby grow,
one day to the next, and think,
this is the closest I will ever get
to bliss, to love, to that elusive peace.

I give him a different name
for every play, every bounce and
every little belly laugh, every single
time he smiles and turns his head away.

His father marvels at the many names
I make up on the spot.

Then, one evening, we are looking at him,
tenderness gushing, time standing still—
a baby sleeping on his tummy, his head
buried between his arms, his squidgy
legs in navy shorts – and we look
to each other, and say what we both
think, what breaks our hearts, what
makes us move closer to each other.
For this, we do not make up names.

Our baby, sleeping, an enactment
of that little boy washed ashore.

Our baby, sleeping, making us mourn.
Our baby, sleeping, and at that moment
we only see Alan, Alan Kurdi, we weep
at a world that failed them all.

THE TRANSMISSION OF POLITICAL IDEOLOGY
~~DOES NOT~~ MAY TAKE PLACE THROUGH
THE EXCHANGE OF BODY FLUIDS

Comrade, take the word austerity.

Where I came from, austerity meant suffering that let you achieve the grand things: paradise, a lover back from the dead, an end to the cycle of birth and rebirth, eternal life, eternal youth. It was only in the English translation of the epics that I ever encountered this word. It was a word that regularly occurred along with, or in place of the word penance. From what I recall of that religious childhood – austerity, at least in the bite-sized versions handed out to us, was associated only with sages and saints, with gods and godheads, with the avatars and incarnations, and with guilt-ridden demons who wanted to turn a new leaf because they hankered after absolvement and the afterlife. It was suffering that let you be seen, let you be heard, that forced the gods to leave their heavenly abodes, leave their cosmic lovemaking, and step down to earth to address pressing concerns.

It was the demon king Ravanan cutting his head as an offering to the god Shiva, night after night, day after day, and the god, tired of having to make it regenerate to let him carry on his penance, granting him ten heads and battlefield invincibility. It was the ageing Bhishman lying on his bed of arrows so that he doesn't have to be born again. It was Kaaman standing on one toe for one thousand years so that the gods would grant him one wish, and he would reply, *could I see my wife again, just one more time?* And they would ponder, and deliberate and arrive at a middle-ground boon, *you can see her, but only you can see her – no one else can*, and he will be pleased, and he will go and live in that state of hallucination. Someone sat on corpses. Someone stared at the sun for days on end. Someone sat in the middle of four blazing fires.

In the way I understood that word as a child, austerity did not come after you to cause you grief or inflict its horrors. It was mortification of the body, self-inflicted suffering that gave you bargaining power with arrogant gods. Stupidity and tenacity were at the heart of this torturous enterprise, but it got things done.

When I first hear the word 'austerity' in this country, the word is not recognizable. It does not wear its wounds with the same flamboyance on this island. I do not see the exaggerated mutilation. Here, it is not some chosen suffering: it seems to denote something held back (benefits), something taken away (meals for school children), several doors closing (downsizing).

These things I see around me, my Tamil girl response labels 'white poverty' but Comrade, I hear you use the austerity word instead, to mean fucked-by-the-system and driven-to-destitution. You turn to diagnosis and pathologizing, as if you were indeed a doctor roaming these streets. When you come back home one day, from the Walthamstow market, you tell me of the shady characters you have seen, of the visibly mentally disturbed, their numbers rising, of a man walking with three white rabbits inside a supermarket trolley, and between the dishevelment that you describe and the word you use for this man: 'austerity victim' – I see a circle struggling to close.

WERE TIME TO HOLD US PRISONERS

Why grudge the time you spend with me, love?

In another birth we will be born even more
apart, we won't know the shape of the other's
face, the colour of the other's skin, the words
for love in the other's tongue, and what it will
mean to spend a night in each other's arms.
Then, only this constant absence of a love we
knew very long ago, a love we can no longer
reach to touch, a love that will betray itself in
tears, a love that will make us weep on full
moon nights. Other loves may take place, take
space, even take away this unnamed pain that
skins our hearts, but only we will know, with the
sureness of old souls, why we long for that part
of us which went missing. Then, we cannot
make claims. I cannot turn up at your door and
ask for a kiss. I cannot even ask for a fight.

Love me now. The torments, of being torn
apart, can haunt us another day.

WE ARE LEARNING BY HEART

We are learning by heart
What has never been taught.
         – Audre Lorde, 'Call'

Take One:

Maggie Nelson claimed blue: its melancholic shades,
its ocean-sky expanse, its laidback coolness – carrying it away,
a cloud cradling a storm, all strength and delicacy.

Before Pantone-onslaughts, before hex triplets, Marx and his
men made off with bloody red.

Like in the children's schoolyard game, the question that
taunts me: 'Colour, colour, what colour do you choose?'

﹡ ﹡ ﹡

Take Two:

Other people,
and their onslaught on cataloguing:

Brent Berlin and Paul Kay examined the colour
terminology of nearly a hundred languages to settle down
on the 11 basic colour categories: white, black, red, green,
yellow, blue, brown, purple, pink, orange and grey.

Another unexpected finding:

If a language encodes fewer than 11 basic colour categories, then there are strict limitations on which categories it may encode. These distributional restrictions are:

1   *All languages contain terms for white and black.*
2   *If a language contains three terms, then it contains a term for red.*
3   *If a language contains four terms, then it contains a term for either green or yellow (but not both).*
4   *If a language contains five terms, then it contains terms for both green and yellow.*
5   *If a language contains six terms, then it contains a term for blue.*
6   *If a language contains seven terms, then it contains a term for brown.*
7   *If a language contains eight or more terms, then it contains a term for purple, pink, orange, grey, or some combination of these.*

✳ ✳ ✳

Take Three:

Like white lies like sly remarks like furtive glances
I'll make my lover an offering of long-held secrets—
colours named in private languages, colours I carry
from where I come, colours living in the moment,
bleed-fade blurring-the-line ones,
dreamlike, direct

in a language old as history,
a language fresh as the fisherman's first catch.

✳ ✳ ✳

Take Four:

What if
we stopped saying whiteness *so it meant* anything.
For example, if you mean milk of magnesia say
milk of magnesia, *or* snow, *or they've hurt another*
one of us, or the quarter-moon is smoke
atop the dirty water, or the pearline damp she laces
up my throat, my face. Mi caracol. *They think*
brown people fuck better when we are sad.

— Natalie Diaz, 'Like Church'

I dig into Tamil, looking for *whiteness*—
the colour of conch-shells, a name for Venus,
and everyone's easy guess: emptiness.
A parasite, it rode on cleanliness & purity,
latched on to brightness & brilliance, light
& lustre. It was also unspeakable shame
speaking for itself: a woman's lovesickness
that left her skin pale; the pallor of illness;
something superficial, never profound;
in poetry, a discordant note or sound;
in people, the ignorant, the guileless,
the one lacking anyone.

Like veneration, violence
followed white everywhere:
Veluveluthal, make *white-white,*
as in, give someone a good thrashing.

✳✳✳

Take Five:

(Wildly, randomly paraphrasing Nicholas Mirzoeff)

For over a century, the search for rational explanations for the irrationality of racial prejudice (social Darwinism) grew strong. Researchers often found what they set to find, so, nineteenth century intellectuals claimed to have identified historical differences in colour perception amongst the different races. Hans Magnus, reading Homer, found a very restricted number of terms for colour. Homer seemed to know his light from dark, but there wasn't much on tints. Magnus concluded that colour sense was a work-in-progress for human evolution.

British Prime Minister Gladstone researched the Odyssey, to find that the idea of colour appeared only once in about a hundred and sixty lines. Homer was High Art so this could not be oversight, he held it was the design construct of a superior civilisation. Gladstone wrote: 'Perhaps one of the most significant relics of the older state of things is to be found in the preference, known to the manufacturing world, of the uncivilised races for strong, and what is called in the spontaneous poetry of trading phrases, loud colour.' In other words, if colour vision was gradual evolution, the least evolved preferred strong, easy-to-distinguish colours because they were still catching up on the civilisational ladder.

Mirzoeff writes, 'All Europeans casually assumed their superiority to other "races," such as Africans, Asians, Jews, who demonstrated that inferiority by their vulgar taste for loud colours.'

✳✳✳

Take Six:

Once, after a terrible fight,
the comrade shouts at me:
'You've shown your true colours.'

I've encountered that expression
a million times before – the blue fox,
the flour-smeared big bad wolf,
amma's admonitions about her
colleagues, my colleagues.

Coming from him, I look at it
in new light: tears skin shame.
He's white, a colour that never
considers itself a colour.
                His first teenage arrest
was at an anti-racism demonstration,
our first kiss at Notting Hill carnival.
'A genuine expression of international
solidarity,' he explained to his comrades:
hapless, encouraging onlookers.
(His credentials are impeccable).

Yet, I feel *showing one's true colours*
means acting as if one were non-white,
means indolence, means a rupture
in a relationship where maybe someone
took you to be someone you were not.

✳✳✳

Take Seven:

Should we show them receipts:
our subtleties, our precision,
our shrewdness is naming,
so that we are counted
evolved, fully human?

Where are the loud colours
in skin the colour of straw,
the burnt clay of terracotta,
earth the colour of a crab's spawn
cloudy pearls the colour of smoky toddy

a moon the yellow-white of jasmine
a gold the yellow-orange of turmeric
a gold taking after some parrot's wing
maturity as in the yellow of ageing

everyday millet named quail's eyes
a palmyra fruit named for dun foxes

lovesickness swallowing skin, turning it
the shade of a sponge-gourd flower

saffron of the saint, of salmon, of
slow-cooking lentils

grey, everywhere in this land,
left without a specific name,
only as an afterthought: ash-coloured

almost everything borrowed
from the nearest object,
never not described.

At every count,
white linguists short-changed—
cursed the natives into conceptions
of innocence – forgive them lord, for they
know not what is being done to them.

✸ ✸ ✸

Take Eight:

Here too, colours wear the skin of stereotype,
black is beauty, vigour and strength, black is freshness
and excellence, the life-giving raincloud, the lord
of the sea, the severe village deity.

black is stain,
repressed rage,
blemish and tarnish both.

dark is the sky growing overcast with clouds,
dark is the dimming of the light,
the luminous body in the faraway
disappearing sky, dark is the one
deprived of lustre, dark is
disappearance

and also,

recurrent, in the arteries of Tamil,
the redness of soil and sunsets and
coral and copper and ochre and
rust and the rice every king paid
as price for his soldier's blood.

YOU, WHO NEVER RUN OUT OF WORDS

(*After Rainer Maria Rilke*)

You, who never run out of words,
Comrade, who bombards me
with endless, numbered arguments.
How do you believe in absolutes
as the seas rise, as ice shelves break,
as spring comes in winter, as monsoon
turns into a torrent of cyclones, as life
halts for years and days resemble
abandoned roads?

Here, life is a roll of dice,
a vagabond's paradise – but you dream
in black and white, punctuate small talk
with your slogans, dazzle us with history
as anecdote, joke, warning.

Broken within,
I ramble to a friend who soon turns lover—
            The comrade, he is my conscience,
    he has my heart but he is unadulterated gold,
    too pure to be a jewel, too soft to hold a gem.
    To his spotless blue sky, I'm a thunderstorm,
    sending forth portents.
We share you like a secret,
I promise to be strong.

In the kitchen, you and I, we hear the radio—
the earth is on fire, the reports say,
and I ask you, unsure, if we did right
in having children, and, for the first time,
Comrade, I catch your silence.

HER LOVERS

A CERTAIN MACKEREL-COLOURED LOVE

Where others sensed scales that
weighed them with every glance,
you only saw the tear-waters
that makes these eyes, fish.
In them, you traced
my shattered temple-roots,
and heard the short-lived,
fish-songs of small seas.

You were given to poetry.

I was given to grand lies—
'Other eyes are mere baits,
yours cast such strong, silken nets.'

In our strange story,
you sought the sea. . .
She swam into you.
With a single lusty fish,
and a certain mackerel-coloured love.

WRITTEN IN STONE

WHAT SHE OFTEN SAID TO HER LOVER

How are you so stone-hearted?
Why this stony-silence?

WHAT HER MOTHER SAID TO HER

What did he say? Did he even react?
Did he commit, did he evade as always?
Was he quiet as the sunken stone
sitting at the bottom of a well?

WHAT HER FATHER SAID TO HER

I love you, my difficult daughter.
I love that you love each other.
Hear me out for I'm an old man:
What will this world say?
Will you be able to face
all their stone-throwing?

WHAT SHE ALSO SAID TO HER LOVER
MANY, MANY YEARS LATER

Those who reject you today
Will tomorrow worship you in stone
There will be your statue in every village
Everyone will name their sons after you.

WHAT HE SAID, ONCE UPON A TIME
BEFORE THEIR STORY EVEN STARTED

From the hardest sun-facing rock,
where there is not a drop of water
sprouts one brave and lonely seed,
sends forth its tiniest leaves,
takes root. It is in the nature
of stone to stay firm, to put
stiff resistance, but faced
with so much tenderness,
such faith, it gives way.

WHAT SHE WROTE AS HER FACEBOOK STATUS
31 AUG 2010

kadhalikka kattru koduthavan
nenjai kallaaga
maatrikkolla,
katru kodukkavillaiye

The one who taught (me)
how to love, did not teach (me)
how to turn my heart
into stone.

This is the nature of love.

This is love.

FIRE WALK WITH ME

Come, walk with me this spring evening
Walk with me as we go past ourselves
We shall change our clothes, we shall paint our faces

Walk with me as we awaken the dead
Walk with me as we disappear into darkness
We shall lock our lips, we shall lock our thighs

Walk with me as we discard this flaming day
Walk with me through this maze of streets
We shall dance to the beat of drums
We shall move to the mad song of our bodies

Walk with me against these blinding lights
Walk with me as we watch the many night-beasts
We shall have forgiven, we shall move as one

Walk with me until we hear the singing of the birds
Walk with me until this night sheds her shameless skin
Walk with me until it is time for my firewalk
Walk with me until it is time to walk away

DIAGNOSED WITH AN AUTO-IMMUNE DISORDER,
I THOUGHT OF MY COUNTRY SELF-DESTRUCTING

forfeiting her future, all our hard-won freedoms,
but that was a worn-out metaphor,
too explicit.

So, I searched for something intimate, like love
turning against itself, like a woman possessed—
a woman, possessive.

    She watched her lover close: eyes like tweezers,
eyes like tongs, eyes like cutting fucking pliers – his layers
were to be plucked and pulled and peeled away,
this'd be the first to go, then that, then his claim
to being faithful, then the lies she told herself
about him, then his easy smile, then the way
he would run to her to share his crazy thoughts,
and then of course, his sadness at the way
the two of them had failed each other.
    She looked on, her eyes falling hammers, her fiery
tongue a sickle to splice him into two & twenty &
a ten thousand with questions that do not let him
hide, that do not let him seek refuge in the truth
he wants to be the truth. . .
    It is my gut that guides me, she said – wrong
all the way, the way the lost remain stranded, the way
the lost get lost and lost – waiting for her lover's fall
from fucking grace, for a heartbreak long overdue,
for that curtain call.

A woman so bitter turns blind.

What fell to the floor
were not his masks, not lies,
not even placeholder love and other crimes.

Staring long enough, she recognised
the old betrayal shrouds she'd dragged
so long to drape her man, heavy,
with the harsh lessons in love
other men left
behind.

A POET GOES IN SEARCH OF A SIDE-CHICK SONG

We go from sexting at midnight
to sharing a hotel bed in another city—
somewhere, a guidebook fills up.
Do not call unless they are alone,
do not leave footprints of your affair
on Twitter, do not save her number
under her first name, do not upload
a thirst selfie as a WhatsApp profile pic,
use an iPhone and encrypted networks,
stay secure, delete transcripts at the end
of every day, do not take selfies together,
stay pokerfaced when his name is dropped. . .
So many precautions, so much delicacy.

This fever-dream we inhabit, I think,
will last so long as the outside world
lies in wait at our doorstep. This, us,
a dew drop on a spider's web – it will stay
untouched, intact, while the world snores,
the sun scratches his eyes, and the wind
contemplates stretching her limbs.

Crafted by night, we will not survive
into the light. We hide away,
we hustle for time. . .

Alone, we make love, we make our own world,
we talk in our mother tongue, we quietly begin
to believe in fate, we watch each other sleep. . .
In your arms, I retire my rebel-girl, stop myself
from bracing for a broken heart.

Dearest, before I wrote this poem,
I scoured the net for a song to send you.

What beats will capture our hearts racing
against these stolen, slow-moving hours?
Where are the lyrics holding a light
to a woman unashamed of having lovers?
Where is the music that comes undone
like me, like us – where are those songs
that don't speak of tomorrows or forevers,
marriages or kids, rattling with promises?
Where are the songs of these moments
we gather in the palm of our hands?
Which chorus heralds our homecoming?

Who will sing to us of the here and now?

THE DISCREET CHARM OF NEOLIBERALISM

In a world that <u>really</u> has been turned on its head,
truth is a moment of falsehood.

       –Guy Debord

We call ourselves poets,
believe our words are weapons
against oppressors, walk around
with bravado for being
such truth-smugglers.

Neoliberalism is not a word
that belongs in any poem, I reason
while I paint my toenails red, wear kohl
and wait for my lover who kisses me,
always, on the eyelids first.

Love births a million poems.
In the restlessness of mine, my lover
sneaks through, a repeat offender,
arriving first in my poems, then
in my arms saying, *ennnadi chellam?*

Neoliberalism knows how to spin, I say:
When workers flock to sweatshops:
the working conditions have improved
and, when workers leave in droves:
the community has been sensitised.

How to spin about a spin master?—
a question I want to ask, but do not.
He kisses me as though all words have been
obliterated—makes love making me birth
afresh a language always, already there.

Days later, we take up where we left off
he says, they have reduced language
to a rotting corpse, and I wince
at the serrated edges of his words.
Neoliberalism finds room in a poem.

YOUR ABSENCE IS A PRESENCE

I wake up with aches I cannot name
to the sound of my younger son,
sat by my side, singing
amma inge vaa vaa…
(the elder, quiet, plays with toy trucks).

The day moves, slow as a centipede,
sure as a checklist: feed, teach, feed,
play, wash, feed, play, feed, sleep—
a monotony only broken by accidents,
illnesses, or, a postman at the door.

Watching my children is like tending a fire:
There is all the warmth in the world, but,
I cannot blink, I cannot turn away.
I've grown a hundred hands,
I've flaming feet.

Eyes open to guard this fire,
your memories come to me
as rain clouds and slanting light.
You are dream and daydream,
you shatter my solitude.
Moist, with stolen kisses
and our suppressed tears,
you wash away my loneliness.

THIS IS ALL WE SHALL EVER HAVE

That we didn't end up with each other
leaves me with a broken heart,
makes you my permanent desire.

Each time I say my regret-filled line:
we never got to share a life together
You retort, rushing to fix my sentence:
this too is together; this too is sharing.

Repeated so often, our respective lines
are now a ritual – I have long forgotten
my once-favourite arguments against it.
Thrown together, we would have
at least had a chance to fail.

Here, we are doomed before we start.
For too long, I wept whole nights.

These days, I dream of a faraway time
where we are born again as birds—
flying under open skies, huddling
under rain-drenched branches—
in this elsewhere we build a nest,
together, we raise our young,
this pain we have harboured
so long, breaks into
beautiful song.

HER FRIENDS

TOMORROW SOMEONE WILL ARREST YOU

(for my close friends Jaison Cooper and Thushar Sarathy, unfairly arrested in 2015)

Tomorrow someone will arrest you. And will say the evidence is that there was some problematic book in your house.

Tomorrow someone will arrest you. And your friends will see, on TV, the media calling you terrorist because the police do.

Tomorrow someone will arrest you. They'll scare all lawyers. The one who takes up your case will be arrested next week.

Tomorrow someone will arrest you. Your friends will find you active on Facebook a day later. Police logged in as you.

Tomorrow someone will arrest you. Your friends will find that it'll take 4 days to find 1000 people to sign a petition.

Tomorrow someone will arrest you. Your little child will learn what UAPA stands for. Your friends will learn of Section 13.

Tomorrow someone will arrest you. You'll be a Leftist to people. You will be Ultra-Left to the Leftists. No one will speak.

Tomorrow someone will arrest you. The day after that, you will be considered a 'terrorist' for life.

Tomorrow someone will arrest you. The police will prepare a list of names. Anyone who'd protest will be named.

Tomorrow someone will arrest you. You'll be warned. You'll be a warning to everyone fighting corporate loot & police state.

Tomorrow someone will arrest you. Your home will be searched tonight. You will be taken for questioning now. Stop speaking.

Tomorrow someone will arrest you. The court, in a rare gesture, will give you the benefit of bail. The police will rearrest you in another case. This will go on and on.

Tomorrow someone will arrest your children. You will be underground. The police will tell your old mother to consume poison and feed it to the kids.

Tomorrow someone will arrest you, your partner, your children, your children's children. Some measures are essential to keep a democracy alive.

Long Live Silence.

SUNSET AT SIEM REAP

(for A)

Looking lost between clouds
this sun is not the lone one
I know from home, the big one
who takes up all the evening sky,
the red one who free falls over tenements,
the drama queen who dips in to dirty
waters when done for the day.
The sun I've known is a star.

Here, this paid-to-perform sun
stays still, delays disappearance,
does not sink until you tame it
into your sonnet about tourists
who trap the sunset with their toys.
Packed into a poem on the spot,
your still sun slowly enters mine and
I too write of foreign, fading light.

Sunset at Siem Reap. A poem
from the comfort of a strange
land, this guilt trip for words
I failed to find at home.

THE OLD TRAP

(for he who is afraid of being named)

It's said one creates for eternity—
We translate our slow rage to strong words

Endlessly annoy Sanghi hate-mongers,
squandering away our talent and time

To write poems with the lifespan of flies—
They pile up as the horrors continue.

Varavara Rao. G N Saibaba.
Poets writing in blood from their cages,

A list that grows on, a list that breaks us.
And soon we write prefaces to their work—

Look! Prison Poetry! Weep! Dissent Writing!
We raise in lament: *Don't kill them in jail!*

This urge to keep chronicling takes its toll
We delete our political selfhood

So much that when a nice man who admires
intelligence almost asks me out,

I blank out. I make a promise: I'll get
really tipsy, I'll look really pretty,

I'll sit there blushing until I gather
the bloody guts to make a move on you.

Courage is in such short supply these days.
Mine, I use it for the war on the streets,

An empty-handed warrior, I waltz
into men, search for the one with a spine.

THEY ARE AFTER ME

(for __,
in the hope that the art will eventually let you heal)

We spent an afternoon watching ferries.
To show me something, you wouldn't point,
or pull me close – you shot it on your phone,

passed it on. I expected beauty – you captured
terror. Sunlight stabbing water, jittery dead leaves,
unseen turbulence shaking tiny worlds into dread.

Cameras were your knives to splice this life. You
knew only to show, not to speak. You were in love
with me, that intense way an artist wants his muse.

Your films were full of unmarried couples fucking,
pretty women chain-smoking, youngsters eloping.
You ticked the coolest box of them all: controversy.

In the beginning, they went after you: a ban; a price
on your head; shunning you from their coteries, their
awards ceremonies. The predators made you prey,

took pleasure in watching you run. They watched you
cut away all your friends, watched you land each step
with no trust, watched you descend into madness.

They made you a tragic movie, artist as art.
Now, you run when no one is chasing.
We call you by your name. Our echoes

fracture mountains, freeze each crashing wave,
but you do not turn back, you do not stop.
You are breathless. You are on the run.

IN LIEU OF AN ARTIST STATEMENT, IN LIEU OF A POEM, IN LIEU OF A DIARY

The year my book came out, a friend told me over drinks,
'Ah! Ms Militancy! You've radicalised a lot of bimbos.'
It seemed to sum up the mainstream opinion about feminist
poetry. In the twelve years since, I did a lot of running –
from men women marriage cities countries politics poetry.

In these intervening years, I wrote a lot. Not poetry. Not
poetry unless I was driven to it by rage or love. Poetry
didn't serve the practical purpose of essays/op-eds; it could
not argue with razor-sharp precision, it did not intervene
in urgent discourse. Poetry did not create a tiny universe
of people, the way novels did. I gave myself to these other
forms.

❋ ❋

Poetry stops, but one does not stop being a poet.
Always, a sadness in these eyes,
Always, this heavy, broken heart,
Always, ready tears and hope.

❋ ❋

I let go of poetry the same year my first lover let go of me.
I moved on to other loves, other lovers.
It remained an electrifying memory.

One does not stop speaking about things
    which no longer exist.
So I would turn up on a stage, read poems.
    I would discuss poetry.

✳ ✳

Beyond the abstractions, what actually happened?
Beyond the gushing fan-mails, what remained?

Beyond the raves of peers, the ABVP agitations,
book-burnings & threats, what would I tell
my grandchildren?

Two stories.

1
A young friend in Kerala told me his cousin-sister
was rejected from a marriage alliance by the man's family
who said: 'She is the kind of woman who reads Meena
    Kandasamy.'

2
A student wrote to me, saying, 'Ma'am, you never taught me
but I went to _____ when you taught there, I follow your work
on Facebook, I come from a Brahmin family, I learnt a lot.
Today, browsing with mum next to me, your post showed up
& she asked, "Hey why do you read this Meena Kandasamy?
Isn't she against Brahmins, isn't she ranting always?
Isn't she now talking about LGBTQ-whatever-whatever?"
                And all I did was smile. I stayed silent.
And amma asked, "Why do you smile? Say something?"
                I smiled again. I said nothing.
And then, she asked, "Are you _____?"

I smiled and she understood.

        Thank you, Meena ma'am
for making my coming out so easy. Love.'

MARTYR

A militant, whom my lines
cannot hold whom my lips
cannot kiss whom my eyes
cannot hide whom my memory
cannot mark with a date
of birth or even death.

No knowledge of her village
laid waste, then displaced and
no mention of her songs
seeking to seize a state and
no sign of a red star where
she had stashed her dreams.

In this book of martyrs
only that blood-drenched
story in three bold words:
'One Woman Comrade'
to say she died fighting
for the people.

WHEN SIXTY (& SOME) WINTERS BESIEGE HIS BROW

What do those wrinkles say?

That you have lived long and seen a lifetime of struggle.
That you spend too much time in thought. That you hide
your sorrows bravely, but they cannot pass unless they leave
a mark on you somewhere, and your forehead is where they
have made a home for themselves, a crease for each tear you
did not shed.

The more years you take, the more they will come, and the
more I will feel how much of yourself you have given away
to this world.

What do they say to me?

That I love you for all your years, that I love you for all
these lives that you are fitting into one, that I love you for all
the fights you wage, that I love you for the world you will
leave behind.

PROCESS = PUNISHMENT

(Dedicated to the Bhima Koregaon – 16)

Some activists dreamed of another world,
demanded paradise, repeated
the same old, the same old:
The people want the fall of the regime
The people want a welfare state
The people want a people's rule
The people want to tax the rich
The people want their children
        clothed & fed & taught. . .
The people want freedom
The people want hope

To silence these sloganeers,
a case was slapped:

      Tukde Tukde Gang x Terror
      Anti-National x Urban Naxal

a staged spectacle, an eclipse shutting out all light,
myths peddled between commercial breaks,
a primetime media circus on loop
like that playground nonsense rhyme
there was a girl so thin so tall so fair

her hair her hair was the colour of ginger
there was a conspiracy to assassinate
the prime minister *there was a girl*
so thin so tall so fair her hair her hair
was the colour of ginger, there was
a conspiracy to destabilise the state
there was a girl so thin so tall so fair
her hair her hair was the colour of ginger
there was a conspiracy to incite violence
there was a girl so thin so tall so fair
her hair her hair was the colour of ginger
truth lay buried under lies, lies buried
within a ten-thousand-page chargesheet

and as in that rhyme, *there was a girl*
so thin so tall so fair her hair her hair
was the colour of ginger, for every two steps
forward, there had to be a step backward

the process endless,
the progress pointless

Now we hear their muffled voices—
pleading in a courtroom drama
oranges & lemons all for a penny
the grass is green the rose is red
remember me when I am dead
dead dead their lawyers
petitioning the small asks
for the small alms,

running around
and around
in circles

a mattress. extra blankets. clothes
pain medication. a tooth extraction.
a biopsy. a copy of old medical records.
a portable commode. the vaccine.
the second dose. the booster dose.
a covid test. clean water. books to read.
letters from home. a laptop to write.
a phone call with ninety-year-old mother.
a straw. a sipper cup.

Do not forget the straw, the sipper cup
for the eighty-four-year-old Jesuit priest
the grass is green the rose is red
remember me when I am dead
dead dead suffering from Parkinson's,
he could not even sign his name
inside the courthouse – but
he died in custody,
undertrial, martyr.
remember me
when I am
dead
dead
dead

Three years since the first arrests,
the others await trial
or death.

❋❋

Our friends in prison,
we meet for the first time

Walking inside a forest,
we try to find words

to remember the dead,
read the heartless future,

and, to my barrage of questions,
you give silence and straight answers,

I walk in step with you,
and watch the leaves fall.

❋❋

remember me when I am dead dead dead
remember me when I am
dead dead dead

HER COUNTRY

SANGHARSH KARNA HAI

(In memory of Jyoti Singh, who died following the heinous rape in New Delhi in December 2012. Sangharsh karna hai, or, 'have to struggle/fight' were her last words)

here, the hurried truth:
day after day after day

of battling death and
keeping him at bay
you became the star
taking struggle in her stride
and we became the body
breaking free, we became
the scream cutting loose
from the curse of silence,
we became the protest
that poured like blood
from a wounded night
and learning from you,
we became the flesh
that became the fight.

HOW TO MAKE A BITCH GIVE UP BEEF

An enumeration of strategies employed against the poet after her defence of the organisers of the 2012 Hyderabad Beef Festival and her condemnation of the subsequent violence.

PLAN ONE: GO FOR GANDHI
Quote the Father of the Nation to prevent the Mother of the Hindus from being eaten by bitches and bastards.

PLAN TWO: GO FOR THE GODDESS
Tell the bitch that Saraswati, the Hindu goddess of learning, will desert the Osmania University campus, outraged that her sister the Holy Cow was cooked and consumed.

PLAN THREE: CALL FOR A CANNIBALISM ALERT
Warn the general public that because the bitch does not mind eating her Mother the Cow she may one day eat her Mother the Human.

PLAN FOUR: INVESTIGATE TERROR LINKS
Accuse the bitch of having links with Hyderabadi and Kashmiri jihadi organizations. And the Tamil Tigers. And of being an enemy agent.

PLAN FIVE: PUT HER BEHIND BARS
Call upon thousands of Hindu legal eagles to file criminal cases against the bitch in every city of India for spreading disharmony or feelings of enmity leading to violence and inciting, provoking and hurting religious sentiments under 153A and 295A of the Indian Penal Code, thus forcing her to waste her whole life in court dates.

PLAN SEX: PUT HER MORALITY AT STEAK

Blame the beef-eating bitch for bashing up her husband. Or, blame the husband for not giving the bitch enough beef, leaving her unsatisfied and fuelling her appetite for forbidden flesh.

PLAN SEVEN: BRING IN ANOTHER ANIMAL

Although it is not anyone's mother, tell the bitch that the Pig from *Animal Farm* can effectively match up to the Indian Holy Cow.

PLAN EIGHT: ALLEGE CORPORATE CONSPIRACY

Dismiss the beef-festival as being a silly episode indirectly funded by a publicity hungry McDonald's. Simultaneously accuse the bitch of being Communist.

PLAN NINE: LAUNCH A 'QUIT INDIA' CAMPAIGN

Ask the bitch to take her caste's share of land as per the British Communal Award and build her own nation where beef-eating can be practised.

PLANTAIN: PROMOTE VEGETARIANISM

Try to convince the bitch of the social, political, ecological, economical and environmental benefits of avoiding meat.

PLAN ELEVEN: ISSUE AN ACID–ATTACK THREAT

Because the bitch is an anti-Hindu Ram-rubbishing terrorist poet and venomous serpent, ask your followers to get carbolic acid concentrate ready.

PLAN TWELVE: ISSUE A GANG–RAPE THREAT
Tweet @beefeatingbitch: 'bloody bitch, u sud be gang-raped
n telecasted live, that will awesome experience.'
Simultaneously, explore the possibilities of an Islamic-style
Hindu fatwa to finish the bitch once and for all.

#THISPOEMWILLPROVOKEYOU

This poem is not a Hindu.
This poem is eager to offend.
This poem is shallow and distorted.
This poem is a non-serious representation of Hinduism.
This poem is a haphazard presentation.
This poem is riddled.
This poem is a heresy.
This poem is a factual inaccuracy.
This poem has missionary zeal.
This poem has a hidden agenda.
This poem denigrates Hindus.
This poem shows them in poor light.
This poem concentrates on the negative aspects of
    Hinduism.
This poem concentrates on the evil practices of Hinduism.
This poem asserts its moral right to use
    objectionable words for Gods.
This poem celebrates Krishna's freedom
    to perch on a naked woman.
This poem flames with the fires of a woman hungry of sex.
This poem supplies sexual connotations.
This poem puts the phallus back into the picture.
This poem makes the shiva lingam the male sexual organ.
This poem does not make the above-mentioned organ erect.
This poem prides itself in its perverse mindset.
This poem shows malice to Hinduism
    for Untouchability and misogyny.
This poem declares the absence of a Hindu canon.
This poem declares itself the Hindu canon.
This poem follows the monkey.

This poem worships the horse.

This poem supersedes the Vedas and the supreme scriptures.

This poem does not culture the jungle.

This poem jungles the culture.

This poem storms into temples with tanks.

This poem stands corrected: the RSS is BJP's mother.

This poem is not vulnerable.

This poem is Section 153-A proof.

This poem is also idiot-proof.

This poem quotes Dr Ambedkar.

This poem considers Ramayana a hetero-normative novel.

This poem breaches Section 295A
    of the Indian Penile Code.

This poem is pure and total blasphemy.

This poem is a voyeur.

This poem gossips about the sex between Sita and Laxman.

This poem is a witness to the rape of Shurpanaka.

This poem smears Rama for his suspicious mind.

This poem was once forced into suttee.

This poem is now taking her revenge.

This poem is addicted to eating beef.

This poem knows the castes of all
    the thirty-three million Hindu Gods.

This poem got court summons
    for switching the castes of Gods.

This poem once dated Karna
    who was sure he was no test-tube baby.

This poem is not curious about who-was-the-father.

This poem is horizontally flipped.

This poem is a plagiarised version.

This poem is selectively chosen.

This poem is running paternity tests on Hindutva.
This poem saw Godse (of the RSS) kill Gandhi.
This poem is not afraid of being imprisoned.
This poem does not comply to client demands.
This poem is pornographic.
This poem will not tender an unconditional apology.
This poem will not be Penguined.
This poem will not be pulped.

RESURRECTION

this poem is for 24-year-old dharmapuri ilavarasan
with three autopsies on your handsome body

this poem is for 29-year-old mudassir kamran
people in kashmir deserve the truth

this poem is for 19-year-old gurvinder singh
yes, it matters if the fascists shot you dead
or drove into you

this poem is for 22-year-old badru mandvi
embalmed in salt & herbs, shrinkwrapped in plastic
by your people who wait for years to clear your name

this poem is for all the parents
who make mighty states tremble
by refusing to bury their sons

※※

the unceasing tears of a father
who cannot even whisper
in his dead son's ears:
suffering is inevitable

the red-hot rage of a mother
who does not stop to mourn
but demands they cut him up
because she knows her son's cold body
holds the truth, holds someone's hate

the silence in the blood
the fading of the stars
and love which makes
a dead young man's family
demand a second autopsy
sometimes, a third

the stillness in the heart
the terror of moonlight in a morgue
this bloody love, a quest for justice—
a parent's broken heart, unsentimental,
letting a dear son survive another mutilation

a chorus to douse the flames
he's dead don't cry he's dead
he's a legend now he's a legend already
our legends don't die

his life was [his love] was his death
his death was [our anger] is our struggle
our struggle is [our love] is our son
somewhere, the words unsaid:
they killed him once already,
they cannot kill our son again.

RAPE NATION

In Hathras, cops barricade a raped woman's home,
hijack her corpse, set it afire on a murderous night,
deaf to her mother's howling pain. In a land where
Dalits cannot rule, they cannot rage, or even mourn.
This has happened before, this will happen again.

What does that fire remember? The screams of satis
dragged to their husband's pyres and brides burnt alive;
the wails of caste-crossed lovers put to death,
the tongue-chopped shrieking of raped women.
This has happened before, this will happen again.

Manu said once, so his dickheads repeat today:
all women are harlots, all women are base;
all women seek is sex, all they shall have is rape.
Manu gives men a licence plate, such rape-mandate.
This has happened before, this will happen again.

This has happened before, this will happen again.
Sanatan, the only law of the land that's in force,
Sanatan, where nothing, nothing ever will change.
Always, always a victim-blaming slut-template,
a rapist-shielding police state, a caste-denying fourth estate.

This has happened before, this will happen again.

INDIA IS MY COUNTRY

Like the fascist who led us to this ruin, death has also learnt to wear a different disguise these days.

No heavy as sorrow rose-marigold garlands, no one tying up the corpse's big toes together, no one folding their rigid hands as if in prayer, no one wrapping them in fresh silk clothes, no freezer boxes attached to power outlets, no one spraying eau-de-cologne so the dead keep fresh through the wake, no one stuffing the ears and nostrils of the corpse with cotton balls, no one fussing about with a coin on the dead one's forehead, no women singing dirges, no women beating their breasts or tearing their clothes, no steady stream of visitors, no howling cries that ripple through the room, no bossy men to say women and children cannot come to graveyards, no cousins poking you in the ribs and saying the next body will fall in your home, no booze, no funeral drums, no pall-bearers, no coffins, no vaikarisi, none of the hysteria we came to associate with death, none of the collective catharsis, none of the never-ending tears

Only the endless sight of anonymous corpses wrapped in white plastic streaming out from ambulances, a lone relative who builds the pyre with a lot of help, rows & rows & rows of open-air pyres with wood mercilessly piled close together to contain the flames, unrepentant fire and ash, cremation workers moving around in that smoky daze, recycling the wood that has not had the heart to burn

On this last journey: no mortal remains, no farewells, no last words

We mourn for the dead,
we mourn for our numbness.

We mourn for the lost pride that let us say each day,
India is my country, and now we feebly add,
my country is a crematorium.

A POET LEARNS THE LIMITATIONS OF HER CRAFT

I am singing a song that can only be born after losing a country.
—Joy Harjo

██████ ████ ████ ████ ████
[Urgent]
This cannot fit into a poem.
This should be a political pamphlet.

█ █████ ████ ██ ███ ███ ████
[Scandalous]
This should be a white paper.

████████!
[Chilling]
This should be the slogans on all our streets.

██████ : ███ ██ ████ █████ ███ ███
[Shameful]
This is apartheid. Who will boycott the boycotters?

██████ █████ ███ ████
[Horror]
This should be a HRW-Amnesty International report.

████████ & █████'██ ████████
[Heartbreaking]
This should be a thoroughly researched documentary film.

████████████████████████████████
[Disturbing]
This should be a long-read in the *New York Times*.

[Haunting]
History will never absolve us.
Their long march home is a story to be told to our future
    generations.

[Oppressive]
When will our political class break its silence?

[Depressing]
When will all the progressive forces unite against Hindutva
    fascists?

[Outrageous]
Why does the state police women's bodies with impunity?

[Devastating]
Such sacrifice!
When will we have our revolution?

[Warning]
The price will always be paid in blood.

What is the use of a poem in this season of hate?
The regular cliches: A desperate cry for help,
an act of witness, a scream into the void?

What is the use of a poet in a season of bloodshed?
Tell me, dear ones. Is she the one who grieves?

Is she the one who guards the embers
of a people's rage?

Is she the one who mirrors
your shattered heart?

Or, is she the one
who speaks to show
she is not yet dead?

WE ARE NOT THE CITIZENS

naamaarkum kudiyallom, namanai anjom
naragathil idar padom, nadalai illom

We are not the subjects of anyone
We do not fear the god of death
We shall not suffer, were we to end in hell
We've no deception, we've no illusions.

naamaarkum kudiyallom, namanai anjom
naragathil idar padom, nadalai illom

Nobody's citizens and nobody's slaves
Fearless of lynchings and beheadings
Unscathed by the torrent of hell-fires
We do not tremble at certain death.

naamaarkum kudiyallom, namanai anjom
naragathil idar padom, nadalai illom

As people, we refuse to be ruled
As people, we refuse to die
As people, we refuse to suffer
As people, we refuse to be deceived.

naamaarkum kudiyallom, namanai anjom
naragathil idar padom, nadalai illom

ENDNOTES

THE SEVEN STAGES

According to popular understanding, the seven stages of love in Arabic literature are **hub** (attraction), **uns** (infatuation), **ishq** (love), **aquidat** (trust/reverence), **ibaadat** (worship), **junoon** (obsession/madness) and **maut** (death).

'Honour killings' are rife in India where death is the punishment doled out to intercaste couples (often, where the man is a Dalit/ex-Untouchable, and the woman is from a dominant/upper caste). Endogamy (marriage across castes) is prohibited in order to preserve the caste system, and lovers who decide to militate against caste codes are punished by death.

✳ ✳

A POEM ON NOT WRITING POEMS

Seen as the first case of killing related to cow vigilantism in India, 51-year-old Akhlaq was lynched in Uttar Pradesh's Dadri district on suspicion of storing beef in his house on 28 September 2015. Akhlaq was dragged from his house and killed by a 200-strong mob of villagers. A BBC report cites his 75-year-old mother Asghari Akhlaq: 'They came from everywhere. Over the walls, through the gate...They just barged into the house, shouting that we had slaughtered a cow.'

Hate politics over the cow, and particularly the eating of beef, has been central to Hindutva.

✳ ✳

THE WARS COME HOME

The arresting image of Alan Kurdi (initially reported as Aylan Kurdi), a three-year-old Syrian boy of Kurdish ethnicity washed ashore in the Mediterranean Sea, jolted the world, and brought to light the utter cruelty of Europe's (and Canada's) policy on refugees and asylum seekers. The toddler was on a boat with 15 others when the boat capsized off Bodrum in Turkey; he drowned along with his mother and brother.

✳ ✳

WE ARE LEARNING BY HEART

The title is taken from a line in Audre Lorde's poem, 'Call'.

The language alluded to in this poem, and from whose ancient words for colours this poem builds itself upon, is my mother tongue Tamil. The colour-references which I have retrieved come from the University of Madras Tamil Lexicon (1936). I thank my friend Reyazul Haque for reading an early draft of this poem, and pointing me in the direction of Mirzoeff's work. This poem was born in 2014, and I finally finished it several years later. I've written elsewhere about Sapir-Whorf's famous hypothesis that our language determines the way we see the world, and here, I played at taking the idea literally, and finding out what happened when all of us embraced a universal way of naming colours. When I started to work on this poem, trying to collect what has been permanently lost/replaced, I had not even heard of the word decolonisation. Part of my inclination was to remember what is forgotten. Part of the urge was to smuggle into English a non-western scheme of looking at, and naming, the world. Part of the tragedy was the realisation that under global mono-culture and uniform Anglophone education, the very way we perceive the world around us has been standardised and homogenised.

I reference Berlin and Kay's work from Dieter B Kapp, *Basic Colour Terms in South Dravidian Tribal Languages*, Indo-Iranian Journal, Vol. 47, No. 3/4 (2004), pp. 193-4, and Mirzoeff's work from Nicholas Mirzoeff, *An Introduction to Visual Culture*, Routledge (2009).

※ ※

WRITTEN IN STONE

In the poem 'Written in Stone', I employ the classical Tamil Sangam poetry tradition of framing love poetry using quoted speech, where several points of view are juxtaposed, creating an intimate world of He Said, She Said, What His Girlfriend Said to Her, and so on. Sangam poetry has an antiquity of over two thousand years, which is the reason for choosing to mimic its structures in this poem, to highlight that love has always had a strife-ridden existence, and that all of love is birthed in this continuum.

Sangam poetry also abounds in rich descriptions of nature and the ecological landscape, and here a woman looks back at her relationship with her lover, remembers all the metaphors that relate to stone, which is at once primeval and enduring. Even as the world outside is turning increasingly sectarian and casteist, and men and women are being killed (honour killings) for daring to love against diktats, this poem seeks to preserve a tiny universe of precious intimacy.

✳ ✳

FIRE WALK WITH ME

This poem imagines the journey of two unlikely lovers on a dark and festive night. It was commissioned to accompany the photographer Vasantha Yoganathan's interpretation of the *Ramayana,* in the section *Trial by Fire* where he has captured the Dusshera festival at Kulasekarapattinam. In this poem, Sita is accompanied by Ravana. The festival at Kulasekarapattinam is about shedding normative identities. I wanted to superimpose the mood of the festival, the centrality it affords to transgender people, and reimagine the Ramayana. In this poem Sita and Ravanan spend time together on their terms in the full knowledge that in the end what awaits her will be the firewalk.

In my last book of poetry, *Ms Militancy*, I retold Hindu and Tamil myths from a feminist perspective. There were poems on the Ramayana (*Traitress*, about Soorpanakai, Ravanan's sister; *Random Access Man*, about Raman; and *Princess-in-Exile* about Sita). For long, I wanted to write a poem on Ravanan from Sita's perspective – exploring both her falling in love with her captor, and also, the possible realisation that he was a better man than the husband she was leaving behind. In most versions of the epic, Ravanan treats her with utmost tenderness. Here I ask the question, what if she gave in, what if she reciprocated? After the trial by fire that she was forced to undergo by Rama in order to accept her back as his wife, would she not have longed to be reunited with someone who treated her with far greater love and respect?

※ ※

THE DISCREET CHARM OF NEOLIBERALISM

This poem takes on the impossibility of wresting language away from neoliberalism's total hijack of it. The examples cited result from my discussions with the Dalit woman leader of a powerful trade union in Tamil Nadu, who was lamenting about the sinister nexus between capitalists and the NGO sector – and how the NGO sector has been deployed to give a positive spin on the havoc wreaked by capitalism. Feminism and the empowerment of women are words easily co-opted by neoliberalism. Democracy, change, people, power – any word with a radical connotation is soon appropriated by neoliberalism. In this milieu, where do we look for a language that does not serve the exploitative ruling class? Can truth only be spoken between lovers? How can a poem – a space where truth is smuggled in for safe-keeping – peel away the hypocrisy of neoliberal onslaught on language, simultaneously reiterating trust in words? The waiting for the lover is symbolic, it signifies that there is still hope for love and truth, even as we live under a devastating economic system.

※ ※

TOMORROW SOMEONE WILL ARREST YOU

This poem grew out of a series of Twitter/Facebook protests immediately following the arrest of my friends Jaison Cooper and Thushar Sarathy under the anti-terrorism law, UAPA, in January 2015. For a close reading of the poem and the political context in which it was written, please refer to 'The End of Tomorrow', an essay on this poem by Manash Firaq Bhattacharjee.

※ ※

THE OLD TRAP

Varavara Rao is an 82-year-old poet who has been imprisoned on false charges of terrorism, inciting violence and a conspiracy to assassinate the Indian Prime Minister in the high-profile Bhima Koregaon case. Three years after his arrest, he still awaits trial. G N Saibaba is a 55-year-old professor of English and poet, who is spending his time in solitary confinement at the Nagpur jail, having been convicted of links with Left-wing extremist organisations. Prof Saibaba suffers from 90% disability, and his family maintains that he has been framed for his criticism of the Indian state.

※ ※

THEY ARE AFTER ME

This poem is dedicated to a close friend driven to paranoia as a consequence of being outspoken and creating work in the shadow of fascism. While I have been intrigued and heartbroken, seeing the effect of living under a repressive regime that bears no tolerance for artists, I also hope that we have the responsibility to chronicle the toll that it has taken on our lives as well as our coping mechanisms.

✳ ✳

MARTYR

Many absences birthed this poem. As a part of my reading/ research on women guerrillas, I came across the PDF of 'Women Martyrs of Indian Revolution: Naxalbari to 2010', containing profiles and life histories of women cadre and leaders of People's War, Maoist Communist Centre and the Communist Party of India (Maoist). For several dozen entries, I was startled by the complete lack of biographical information – and realised that in the complex process of remembering, one encounters both erasure and self-erasure. This is a common feature for women militants across the world, including the Tamil Tigers whose struggle I have followed closely. The obliterary nature of war and the taking up for a nom de guerre ensure that their origin stories and event-laden lives are lost from collective memory. This poem was written several years ago.

✳ ✳

WHEN SIXTY (& SOME) WINTERS BESIEGE HIS BROW

The title, if not some of the theme, of this poem is an obvious nod to Shakespeare's Sonnet II, 'When Forty Winters Shall Besiege Thy Brow'.

✳ ✳

SANGHARSH KARNA HAI

This poem was written for *The Hindu* on the passing of Jyoti Singh, the young woman in Delhi who succumbed to a gang-rape in December 2012. Her death was a flash-point in bringing out the unsafe nature of all spaces for Indian women, but it was also the first time that we, as Indian women, could start articulating words like rape within our own drawing rooms. The extreme brutality that was visited upon her and the surge of protest that followed broke the silence and taboo which surrounded the discussion of sexual violence in India.

✳ ✳

HOW TO MAKE A BITCH GIVE UP BEEF

All tweets used in this poem are real.

✳ ✳

#THISPOEMWILLPROVOKEYOU

Wendy Doniger's book *The Hindus: An Alternative History* had been the subject of a legal challenge claiming the text was offensive to Hindus. Hindu campaign group Shiksha Bachao Andolan brought a civil case in 2011 against Penguin India, arguing that the book contained 'heresies' insulting to Hindus leading to the publisher recalling the book. This poem was written in response to the episode, and talks about what is really offensive? The scrutiny of so-called sacred texts or the injustice/inequality structurally embedded in their caste-patriarchal ideology?

✳ ✳

RESURRECTION

2012. Tamil Nadu

Ilavarasan, a young Dalit man falls in love and marries a dominant caste (Vanniyar) woman, Divya. The intercaste marriage outrages Vanniyars; more than 268 homes of Dalit people in three villages across the Dharmapuri district are burnt to ashes by caste-fanatic mobs enjoying complete police protection on 7 November 2012. A year later, on 4 July 2013, Ilavarasan is mysteriously found dead on the railway tracks along with a handwritten suicide note. The first autopsy was conducted on the following day by a team of three doctors at the Government Medical College Dharmapuri. The second autopsy is conducted by two forensic experts from Chennai, one of whom says in an interview: 'Even if we don't have enough to prove that Ilavarasan was murdered, we have enough to show that he did not commit suicide.' The family and Dalit parties like the VCK hold the view that he was murdered and then thrown before a running train. They approach the Madras High Court, which orders a third autopsy with a team of experts flying in from the All India Institute of Medical Sciences. A total of 12 doctors are involved and three autopsies take place. A forensic expert alleges that 'evidence was tampered with and suppressed – particularly the mysterious appearance of grease marks on the dead youth's chest after two post mortems had already been conducted, presumably to suggest he had made physical contact with the train'. (*The Wire*)

2013. Hyderabad/Kashmir

Mudassir Kamran, a 29-year-old Kashmiri PhD, is found hanging in his room in the English and Foreign Languages University, Hyderabad, India. Regional reports insinuate he is a homosexual tormented by his obsession with another student. In Kashmir, he is called a martyr who has suffered a mysterious death. 20,000 people attend his funeral prayer, local leaders allege that his body bore torture marks, there are widespread demands for a second post-mortem by Kashmiri doctors. (*Kashmir Life*)

2021. Lakhimpur Kheri, Uttar Pradesh

At the peak of the farmers protest, on 3 October 2021, a jeep belonging to a Union Minister's son drove through peaceful protestors killing three of them on the spot. The family of 19-year-old Gurvinder Singh demanded a repostmortem on his body, maintaining that he did not die from the vehicle-ramming violence but from being shot dead by a member of the minister's son's team. (*Telangana Today*)

2022. Chhattisgarh

From a Hindustan Times news-report: 'On March 19, 2020 morning, the Chhattisgarh Police said a Maoist was killed by a joint team of security forces out on counter-insurgency patrol in a gunfight deep in Bastar's Dantewada forest. They said the dead man, Badru Mandvi, was a member of the west division of Maoists in Bastar. Once the formalities were completed, the 22-year-old's body was handed over to his family. Tribals in Kirandul's Gampur village contested the police version that Badru Mandvi was a Maoist, and embalmed the body in the hope that some authority will agree to order an inquiry into Badru Mandvi's killing. That was 23 months ago. Since then, Badru's body is kept in a pit, around 200meters from the village's hutments, wrapped in white shroud and plastic. The tribals smeared the body with salt and some herbs to try to embalm the body.' (*Hindustan Times*)

✳ ✳

RAPE NATION

Written in the immediate aftermath of the gang-rape and murder of a young Dalit woman in Hathras, I was channelling my hopelessness and outrage. For me it was important to tie up the sexual violence and caste atrocity which unfolds in the physical realm with the ideological violence which is already in existence in the collective psyche. For more on the context in which this poem was written and how the poem carries out the task of bearing witness, please read Chinki Sinha's brilliant cover-story in *Outlook* magazine. *Sanatan* here refers to Sanatana Dharma, the word that rightwing Hindus use to self-refer to their religion. It means unchanging and eternal. A key text, *Manusmriti*, has this to say about women in its ninth chapter. It pretty much sums up the outlook towards women:

1. '*Swabhav ev narinam...*' – 2/213. It is the nature of women to seduce men in this world; for that reason, the wise are never unguarded in the company of females.

2. '*Avidvam samlam...*' – 2/214. Women, true to their class character, are capable of leading astray men in this world, not only a fool but even a learned and wise man. Both become slaves of desire.

3. '*Matra swastra* ...' – 2/215. Wise people should avoid sitting alone with one's mother, daughter or sister. Since carnal desire is always strong, it can lead to temptation.

※※

INDIA IS MY COUNTRY

Written during the second wave of the Covid-19 pandemic, this poem captures how crematoriums and burial grounds in the country were conducting mass cremations night and day, overwhelmed with bodies.

The poem owes its visual material to some of the images and video captured by the slain photojournalist Danish Siddiqui. Death rituals are an integral part of cultural practices in the subcontinent, and the poem meditates on their sudden absence.

Vaikarisi is the Tamil custom of feeding rice to the corpse, a farewell ritual.

The title of this poem comes from the everyday school pledge taken by Indian children: *India is my country. All Indians are my brothers and sisters.*

※ ※

WE ARE NOT THE CITIZENS

naamaarkum kudiyallom, namanai anjom
naragathil idar padom, nadalai illom

These are lines from the classic Tamil poetry of the Bhakti poet Thirunaavukkarasar (Appar), who was persecuted by Mahendravarman, the Jain Pallava emperor, for his faith in Shaivism. It's widely believed that these lines were sung when efforts were made to arrest him and produce him in Mahendravarman's court. Because the seventh-century Tamil of Appar is still in use – and at the same time, some words have fallen out of the everyday vocabulary – it opens up to all of these renderings, all of these translations. This declaration, that we are not citizens/subjects, is a radical slogan to throw in the face of the state. In today's world rife with the refugee crisis these words resonate... It encapsulates the people's rejection of a state, and closer home, brings to mind the poet/writer's disowning of association with a state.

This poem is written in response to the times when any critique of the government faces the charge of sedition and the label of anti-national. The poem comes into being just as citizenship laws are used by the Hindu rightwing dispensation to create second class citizens, and to strip people of citizenship.

ACKNOWLEDGEMENTS

Hope is possible because of my two little sons: Z & A, and my comrade: Cedric. Perhaps I go to poetry when I am falling apart, so, here is to the women who hold me together: Nimmi, Kammy, Laura, Prachi. Thanks to Jhansi and Datchayani, two marvellous babysitters who managed to let me escape motherhood for a few hours every week during the pandemic years.

Thanks to my agent David Godwin, and Philippa Sitters at DGA. At Atlantic Books, thanks to everyone for reposing such faith in my work. Special thanks to James Roxburgh and Kirsty Doole. Thanks to my poetry editor, Joanna Lee for her patient reading and her brilliant insight. For the marvellous cover design of this book, my thanks are due to Alice Marwick.

Individual poems have appeared (or are forthcoming in) *Adi Magazine, Gallerie, Islands Are But Mountains* (Platypus Press), *Muse India, Indian Literature, The Obliterary Journal/ Blaft Publications, The Hindu, Outlook Magazine, The Wire, Punch Magazine, Walleah Press, Guftugu/ Indian Cultural Forum, Cordite Poetry Review, Poetry London, The White Review.*